Fun with

M000235051

by Robert R. O'Brien
illustrated by Kenneth Batelman

Harcourt

Orlando   Boston   Dallas   Chicago   San Diego

Visit *The Learning Site!*
www.harcourtschool.com

Introduction

People love the idea of robots. Whether it is a kid sorrowfully trying to avoid chores or a scientist trying to experiment in space, people imagine a robot could do the hard work for them.

Machines have been doing work for people for hundreds of years. However, the idea of a machine that a human could order to work is only about eighty years old. In 1920, an author wrote a play about machines. They would do the kind of work that nobody else wanted to do. He called them *robots*,

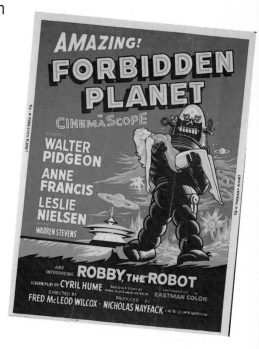

from the Czech word *robota,* which means "forced labor." At the start of the play, the robots were only machines. When a scientist tried to make them more like humans, they tried to take over the world!

Robot Fiction

For many years, robots existed only in fiction. The idea of inventing working robots didn't become popular until the 1940s. That was when people first started to hear about computers. The idea that machines could "think" faster than humans was exciting. People wondered if someday humans could invent a machine that could think on its own.

Many people were worried about what might happen if there were robots in the world.

Scary stories about robots from outer space were very popular. People wondered whether robots would be created that could harm people.

In the 1940s, Isaac Asimov wrote that someday robots would be able to help people. He was the person who made up the term *robotics*. He also drew up Laws of Robotics for building and designing robots:

1. A robot may not injure a human being. It may not allow a human being to come to harm.

2. A robot must obey the orders given to it by human beings, except where such orders would conflict with the First Law.

3. A robot must protect itself, as long as doing so does not conflict with the First or the Second Law.

The kind of robot Asimov described in his laws does not exist. The three laws assume that robots can think on their own. Robots who can think have not yet been invented. All robots designed today get their orders from humans. Robots might be directed by software. They might be directed by radio control. They might be directed from sensors on the robot. However, they can do only what humans tell them. It will be many years before robots that think will be built.

That hasn't stopped people from imagining robots that have minds of their own. Robots have been popular in movies, books, and TV. Sometimes they are good characters that help humans. Other times they are evil characters that try to harm humans. Yet, whether it is a brainy robot that solves the world's problems or some nasty robot from outer space, robots that think are still fiction.

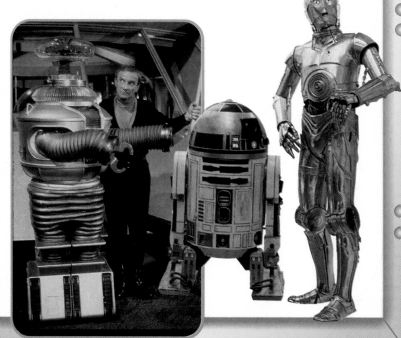

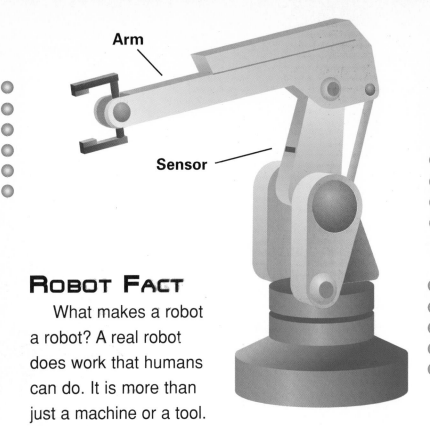

Arm

Sensor

Robot Fact

What makes a robot
a robot? A real robot
does work that humans
can do. It is more than
just a machine or a tool.
A machine or tool is
directly controlled by a human. A robot has a set of
instructions built into its design. Then it can be left
alone. It does its job without being run by a human.

The robot relies on sensors. Humans use their
eyes, ears, nose, tongue, and skin as sensors. For
a robot to work, it must use sensors to help it do its
job. Building a robot means figuring out how the
robot will use sensors to "know" what to do.

The first industrial robot went to work in 1962. It was used in a General Motors plant to help build cars. It had one job. It cooled off car parts so that people could work on them. It picked up hot metal car parts and dunked them in a tank of water.

The dunking job was too dangerous for people to do. The robot did the job without putting any human workers in danger. It was a simple job. It was also the perfect job for a robot to do. The robot performed the job so well that people looked for other ways to use robots in factories.

Now robots are used in all sorts of industries. For many jobs that are very risky, robots are the perfect answer. One way robots have been used is in exploring space. It is currently too dangerous and expensive to send a human to a distant planet. Instead, scientists have sent robots to explore.

The robots that have been sent into space have helped scientists. They have measured temperatures and gases. They have taken pictures of places humans haven't ever seen. They have even gathered rocks and soil samples to send back to Earth.

One of the projects that scientists are working on is a robotic astronaut. This "robonaut" would replace astronauts on space walks.

A walk in space is very dangerous and expensive. A human needs a special suit, a constant air supply, and safety gear. It takes a human astronaut a long time just to get ready to leave the space vehicle.

A robot can be sent out to do the same job. Scientists have built a working robonaut model already. It can be controlled by an astronaut inside the space vehicle.

Robot Fun

Of course, robots don't belong only in factories and in space. Because the cost of robotic parts has dropped, more people are building robots. Smaller electric motors make it possible to make small robots. So people are building robots for personal use.

These home robots can't do very many useful things yet. Industrial robots do one or two jobs over and over. Robots in the home would be expected to do hard jobs, like cooking and cleaning. So far, most robots for home use are not much more than toys.

There are kits you can buy today to build your own small robot. Some kits are very simple. Some allow you to run the robot with a radio controller. Others give the robot the ability to roam around the house on its own.

These robots use sensors to recognize when they are about to hit something. If they bump into an object, they back up and turn. Some can be "trained" to follow their owners around the house, like a mechanical pet.

Robot Games

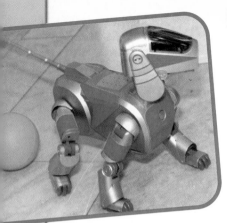

A group of scientists and students in 35 countries have designed small robots that play Robot World Cup soccer. Soccer robots began as a design challenge for college students and others interested in robots. The idea is to do robot research by practicing on small, fun, soccer robots. Someday soccer-robot inventors hope to create a team of robots that will play the best human soccer teams!

The Small Division soccer robots play on a soccer field the size of a Ping-Pong table. There are three robots to a team. The robots try to place a golf ball inside their opponent's goal. They also have to defend their own goal. They are designed to do these things without being directly controlled by a human.

A soccer robot has to be able to follow the ball. It has to be able to move the ball quickly and keep it from being stolen by the robots on the other side. It has to be strong enough to withstand hard knocks. All of its controls have to be adjusted for the best performance. Most of all, it has to be reliable. If your robot breaks down in the middle of a game, you lose!

What do the designers of soccer robots hope to learn from their games? One important goal is to make robots for search and rescue. These robots would be designed to do things like finding people lost during earthquakes or cleaning up dangerous chemical spills.

Robots of the Future

Some people believe that it will be many years before we have real robots that can think on their own. Some people think that it will be a great day when robots become truly useful.

Others dispute that idea. They wonder what will happen if robots start to do the jobs that people do now. In some ways this has happened already. If robots get better, smarter, and cheaper, they will have a huge impact on everyday life.

A robot has been built that will flip hamburgers and cook french fries. What would happen if all of the fast-food meals were cooked by robots? Would the workers who now cook those meals be able to find other jobs?

Some people predict a future when people will depend more on robots to do work around the house. Others loftily dismiss this idea. They don't believe that robots will ever be the kind of helpers that Isaac Asimov and others have predicted. They can't imagine humans nonchalantly turning over certain jobs for thinking machines to do. Some scientists predict a future in which robots will be very common at work and at home. These robots will be very different from the robots that people have imagined so far.

Perhaps one day you will become a robot designer. Maybe you will learn to program the computers that operate robots. Maybe you will learn to build or repair robots. Perhaps you will design a robot that performs delicate brain surgery. There will certainly be lots of jobs in the robot industry for people who understand math, electronics, computers, and how human beings think. One day you might be the person who invents the kind of robot people have always dreamed about.

One thing is certain. Robots are here to stay. They are no longer just an idea in a science fiction story. Robots will change the way we work, live, and play.

16